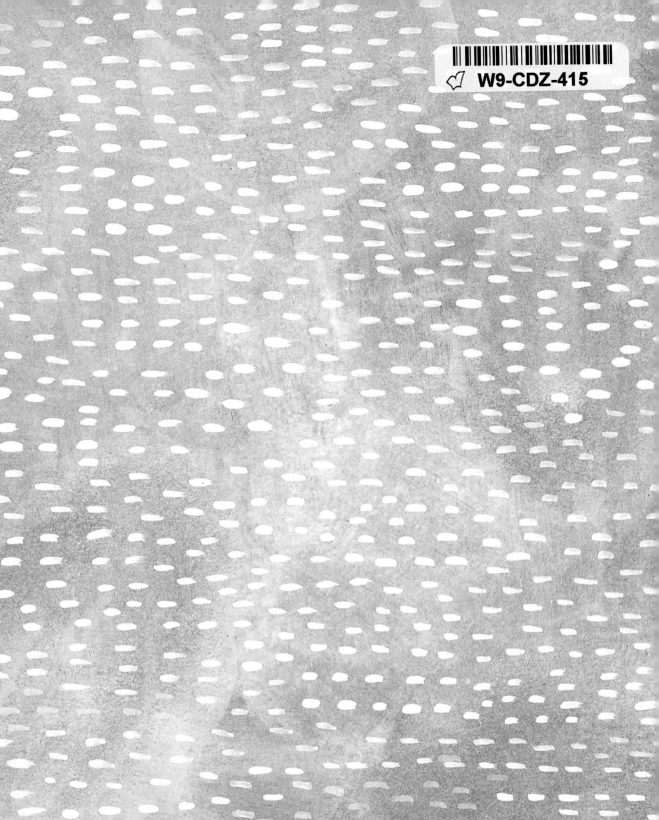

An Island Grows

By Lola M. Schaefer

Illustrated by Cathie Felstead

Greenwillow Books
An Imprint of HarperCollinsPublishers

Deep, deep
beneath the sea . . .

Stone breaks.

Water quakes.

Magma glows.

Volcano blows.

Lava flows

and flows

and flows.

An island grows.

Rocks appear,
    black and sheer.

Weather batters.
    Rock shatters.

Waves pound.
Sands mound.

Winds sow
seeds that blow.

Roots grow.
Leaves show.

Trees tower.
Vines flower.

Insects thrive.
Birds arrive.

Sailors spot.

Maps plot.

Ships dock.

Traders flock.

Settlers stay.
Children play.

Workers build.
Soil is tilled.

Markets sell.
    Merchants yell.

"Fresh fish!"
    "Pepper dish!"

"Ripe fruit!"
"Spicy root!"

Bells ring.
Voices sing.

Drums play.
Dancers sway.

where only water used to be.

Then, one day, not far away,

deep beneath the sea,

a volcano blows,
and lava flows.

Another island grows.

. . . And Now, a Few Details about How Volcanic Islands Grow

Scientists believe that Earth's crust is formed of plates of thick rock. These plates move at the same speed that your fingernails grow. When these plates overlap or pull away from one another, it creates a weak spot in the crust.

Magma is hot, liquid rock inside the planet. It is always pushing upward, like steam in a teakettle. When a weak spot or opening occurs in the crust, magma is forced outward. It usually escapes through the vent of a volcano, like steam forcing its way out of the teakettle's spout. Magma is called *lava* when it flows on Earth's surface. When lava cools, it turns into solid rock.

A volcanic island forms when an undersea volcano erupts. The lava flows into the sea, cools, and becomes rock. Each new layer of lava builds upon the others. A mountain of rock grows so tall that it can be seen as an island in the sea. If the lava flows continue, the island grows larger and larger.

Earth's plates continue to move and eventually cover that weak spot in the crust. At the same time, the plates' movements expose other weak spots. Over many years, this activity can form a chain of islands around the edge of one plate. The Aleutian Islands in southwestern Alaska were made in this way. More than 150 islands have appeared there because of undersea volcanic eruptions.

Volcanic islands can form slowly. The Hawaiian Islands are volcanic islands that have been growing for millions of years. Some of the islands still have erupting volcanoes that continue to add new lava and change the islands' shape.

At other times, a volcano can make an island quickly. In 1963, an undersea volcano began to erupt off the southern coast of Iceland. It continued for two years. When the eruption stopped, the mountain of lava rock had formed a new island called Surtsey.

After a volcano stops erupting, waves and weather erode the rock into loose gravel and sand. Wind, insects, and birds bring seeds, and plants begin to grow. Then other animals such as sea turtles, fish, or seals visit the island. Eventually, people discover and explore the new land. Some stay and build homes. The island is named and becomes its own unique place on Earth.

If you'd like to read more about volcanic islands, visit your local library and ask for these books:

Hawaii Volcanoes National Park, by Sharlene P. Nelson, Scholastic Library Publishing, 1998.

Surtsey, the Newest Place on Earth, by Kathryn Lasky, Hyperion, 1992.

Two Tales of Hawaii, by Terry Pierce, Island Heritage, 2003.

Galapagos: Islands Born of Fire, by Tui DeRoy, Swan Hill Press, 2001.

For Leah and Spencer
—L. M. S.

For Biddy and Erasmus Barlow
—C. F.

An Island Grows. Text copyright © 2006 by Lola M. Schaefer. Illustrations copyright © 2006 by Cathie Felstead. All rights reserved.
Manufactured in China. www.harperchildrens.com
Paper collages were used for the full-color art. The text type is Clichee.
Library of Congress Cataloging-in-Publication Data Schaefer, Lola M. An island grows / by Lola M. Schaefer ; illustrated by Cathie Felstead.   p.   cm.
"Greenwillow Books." Summary: An island is born and as it grows, lava flows, waves pound, and sands mound as the island becomes inhabited.
ISBN-10: 0-06-623930-3 (trade bdg.) ISBN-13: 978-0-06-623930-9 (trade bdg.) ISBN-10: 0-06-623931-1 (lib. bdg.) ISBN-13: 978-0-06-623931-6
[1. Islands—Fiction. 2. Stories in rhyme.] I. Felstead, Cathie, ill. II. Title. PZ8.3+ 2006 [E]—dc22 2005052645
First Edition 10 9 8 7 6 5 4 3 2 1   Greenwillow Books